Angela Cleveland

Choosing the Church

Anabaptist Origins and the Formation of Mennonite Identity

Angela Cleveland

Copyright © 2026 Angela Cleveland

All rights reserved.

No part of this book may be reproduced, stored in a retrieval system, or transmitted in any form or by any means electronic, mechanical, photocopying, recording, or otherwise—without the prior written permission of the author.

ISBN: 979-8-9923815-4-2

DEDICATION

For those who inherit a past

they must still decide how to carry.

TABLE OF CONTENTS

Introduction: Choosing the Church in an Age Without Choice..................7

Chapter 1: Scripture, Literacy, and Religious Dissent....................11

Chapter 2: Infant Baptism and the Meaning of Salvation....................17

Chapter 3: Zurich and the First Anabaptists....................23

Chapter 4: Martyrdom as Proof of Faith....................29

Chapter 5: Münster and the Limits of Reform....................35

Chapter 6: From Priest to Anabaptist Leader....................41

Chapter 7: Voluntary Faith and the Separation of Church and State...47

Chapter 8: Nonresistance and Survival....................53

Chapter 9: Worship, Symbols, and Daily Practice....................59

Chapter 10: Gender, Dress, and Authority....................65

Chapter 11: Discipline and Community Boundaries....................69

Chapter 12: Why Mennonites Divide....................73

Chapter 13: Amish, Hutterites, and Mennonite Brethren....................77

Chapter 14: Why Mennonites Write Memoirs....................81

Chapter 15: Conversion as Crisis....................87

Chapter 16: War, Displacement, and Identity....................93

Chapter 17: Inheriting a Religious Past....................99

Conclusion: Continuity Without Coercion....................105

Note on Sources....................109

Works Referenced.................... 111

About The Author....................113

Introduction: Choosing the Church in an Age Without Choice

In early modern Europe, religious belonging was assigned at birth and enforced by law, leaving little space for personal belief. To be born within a territory was to inherit its church, its theology, and its rituals. Baptism shortly after birth marked not only spiritual inclusion but civic belonging. To reject the church of one's birth was therefore not a private spiritual decision but a public challenge to the foundations of European society.

The Anabaptist movement emerged within this context. Its defining insistence that baptism follow conscious belief directly undermined assumptions about inherited religious identity and civic belonging. By separating faith from birth and belief from citizenship, Anabaptists called into question the legitimacy of both ecclesiastical authority and the political systems that depended upon it. The consequences were severe. Across Europe, Anabaptists were imprisoned, exiled, and executed, not only for theological dissent but for the perceived social instability their ideas introduced.

This book examines how one stream of that movement, later identified as Mennonite, developed in response to persecution, fragmentation, and the persistent problem of sustaining a voluntary church within coercive societies. Rather than presenting Mennonite history as a unified or linear tradition, this book traces a series of contested decisions concerning belief, belonging, discipline, and authority.

The origins of Anabaptism are inseparable from broader transformations underway in Europe during the fifteenth and sixteenth centuries. The spread of print culture expanded access to scripture and theological debate beyond clerical elites. Literacy, while limited, was no longer confined to monasteries and universities, and oral transmission of printed material further extended its reach. These changes contributed to increasing scrutiny of ecclesiastical practices, including indulgences, sacramental mediation, and clerical privilege. Reformers across Europe challenged church authority, though most sought reordering within existing structures rather than their rejection.

Anabaptists moved beyond these limits. They insisted that faith required personal understanding, public confession, and voluntary commitment. Infant baptism, long regarded as both a spiritual safeguard and a civic necessity, was rejected as unscriptural. In its place, Anabaptists emphasized adult baptism as the visible marker of conversion. This position placed them in conflict not only with Roman Catholic authorities but also with emerging Protestant state churches, which retained infant baptism as a foundation of social cohesion.

In territories where religious reform was supported by civic leaders, church and state remained closely intertwined. Refusal to baptize infants or participate in mandated religious practices was interpreted as defiance of communal responsibility. Even Anabaptist groups that rejected violence and political rebellion were viewed as destabilizing forces. Their emphasis on voluntary faith was perceived as incompatible with the legal and social order of the time.

In the early 1530s, the city of Münster became the site of a dramatic and violent episode that reshaped how Anabaptism was understood across Europe. Amid political instability and religious reform, a group of apocalyptic leaders claimed Münster as the divinely chosen "New Jerusalem" and seized control of the city. They enforced adult baptism, expelled dissenters, and imposed sweeping social and religious regulations in anticipation of Christ's imminent return. The experiment ended in siege, famine, and military defeat, followed by the public execution of its leaders. Although the movement in Münster differed sharply from the nonviolent Anabaptist communities emerging elsewhere, its collapse allowed authorities to portray all Anabaptists as inherently dangerous. For those committed to voluntary faith and nonresistance, Münster became a defining crisis that required explicit rejection of coercion and a renewed emphasis on discipline, restraint, and communal accountability.

It was within this fractured and dangerous environment that Menno Simons emerged as a central figure. A former Catholic priest, Simons did not found a new movement so much as organize and stabilize existing Anabaptist communities. His leadership emphasized voluntary faith, strict church discipline, separation from the state, and a theology of nonresistance. Under his influence, scattered congregations developed shared practices and a collective identity that distinguished them from both state churches and radical Anabaptist factions. Over time, these communities came to be known as Mennonites.

Mennonite identity, however, was shaped by more than doctrine. From its earliest formation, it was informed by memories of persecution, martyrdom, exile, and survival. These experiences influenced religious practice, attitudes toward authority, and boundaries between community and world. As Mennonites migrated across Europe and later to Russia, Canada, and the Americas, they carried with them a historical consciousness that linked present faith to past suffering.

This book approaches Mennonite history through two complementary lenses. The first is historical, tracing the development of Anabaptist belief and Mennonite community formation from the sixteenth century onward. The second is interpretive, examining how Mennonites have narrated their own past through memoirs, diaries, and conversion accounts. These narratives illuminate how individual religious decisions are situated within a collective history and how the act of choosing the church continues to shape Mennonite identity across generations.

Choosing the Church does not seek to evaluate the validity of Mennonite belief or to advocate for its practices. Instead, it examines the historical conditions that made voluntary faith both possible and costly, and the ways Mennonites have understood and remembered that choice. By situating personal conversion within a broader historical framework, the book presents Mennonite identity as a continuing negotiation between conscience, community, and history.

Chapter 1: Scripture, Literacy, and Religious Dissent

The emergence of Anabaptism cannot be understood apart from the changing relationship between ordinary believers and religious authority in late medieval Europe. For centuries, the Roman Catholic Church functioned as the primary interpreter of scripture, theology, and religious practice. While personal devotion existed, doctrinal understanding was mediated almost exclusively through clergy. The Bible itself was inaccessible to most laypeople, both because of low literacy rates and because scripture circulated primarily in Latin, a language reserved for ecclesiastical and scholarly use.

By the fifteenth century, this arrangement was under increasing strain. Dissatisfaction with clerical privilege, corruption, and perceived moral laxity was widespread, even among those who remained committed to the Church's authority. Lay religious movements emphasizing personal piety, moral reform, and direct engagement with scripture appeared across Europe. These movements did not initially seek separation from the Church but reflected a growing desire for religious authenticity grounded in personal understanding rather than institutional mediation.[1]

The invention of movable type printing in the mid fifteenth century accelerated these developments. Printed texts made scripture, sermons, and theological commentary more widely available than manuscript culture had allowed. Although literacy rates remained limited, printed material circulated beyond literate elites through oral reading and public recitation. Printed pamphlets and books were read aloud in marketplaces, homes, and informal gatherings, allowing religious ideas to spread across social boundaries.[2]

This expanding access to religious texts encouraged critical engagement with established doctrine. Readers and listeners compared scripture to the practices they observed in church life and noted discrepancies between biblical narratives and institutional traditions. Questions emerged concerning indulgences, sacramental authority, and the role of clergy as intermediaries between God and believers. While these questions did not immediately produce organized dissent, they created conditions in which challenges to ecclesiastical authority could gain traction.

Reform movements that emerged in the early sixteenth century capitalized on this climate of inquiry. Figures such as Martin Luther and Ulrich Zwingli criticized specific church practices while retaining a commitment to reforming Christianity within a structured ecclesiastical framework. Their critiques addressed issues of authority, salvation, and scripture, but they did not reject the close relationship between church and civic governance that characterized European society. In territories where reform succeeded, state-supported Protestant churches replaced Catholic institutions, but religious conformity remained compulsory.

To reject infant baptism was therefore to challenge the assumption that religious belonging was both inherited and enforced, a challenge whose theological implications would later be fully articulated by Anabaptist thinkers. Central to this divergence was the question of baptism. Infant baptism functioned as a cornerstone of religious and civic identity. It marked inclusion in the Christian community and signaled submission to communal authority. To reject infant baptism was therefore to reject not only a sacrament but also the assumption that religious belonging was inherited and involuntary.

The implications of rejecting infant baptism extended far beyond theology, a theme explored in greater detail in the following chapter.[3] Baptism was understood not as a mechanism for removing inherited sin but as a public declaration of faith following conversion. Baptism thus became a visible act of dissent, redefining religious identity as a matter of voluntary allegiance rather than inherited status.

This understanding redefined salvation as contingent upon moral accountability rather than sacramental timing. It also disrupted the legal and social order. In a system where church membership and civic belonging were intertwined, refusal to baptize infants threatened the mechanisms through which communities maintained cohesion. Authorities interpreted Anabaptist beliefs as socially destabilizing regardless of whether adherents advocated political rebellion.

Early Anabaptists did not initially identify themselves by a shared name. The term "Anabaptist," meaning rebaptizer, was applied by opponents and carried a derogatory connotation. Rebaptism was classified as heresy under imperial law and punishable by death. The label itself reinforced perceptions of extremism and provided legal justification for persecution.[4]

Opposition to Anabaptism was swift and severe. Both Catholic and Protestant authorities viewed the movement as a threat to public order. Legal codes criminalized rebaptism, unauthorized preaching, and refusal to participate in state churches. Punishments ranged from imprisonment and exile to execution. These measures were intended to suppress dissent, yet they often reinforced Anabaptist convictions. Martyrdom came to be understood by believers as evidence of faithfulness rather than error.

The willingness of Anabaptists to suffer punishment without resistance further distinguished them from other reform movements. Many rejected the use of violence, refused military service, and declined to swear oaths of allegiance. These positions were grounded in scriptural interpretation rather than political theory, but authorities interpreted them as signs of disloyalty. The refusal to swear oaths, in particular, undermined legal systems that depended on sworn testimony and allegiance.[5]

By the early 1520s, Anabaptist ideas began to coalesce into identifiable communities, particularly in Swiss territories influenced by Zwingli's reform efforts. In Zurich, debates over baptism exposed tensions between reformers who sought gradual change and those who insisted on immediate conformity to scripture. When civic authorities intervened to enforce infant baptism, dissenters faced a choice between submission and separation.

This choice marked a turning point. Those who proceeded with adult baptisms did so in defiance of both ecclesiastical and civic authority. Their actions transformed theological disagreement into lived dissent. From this point forward, Anabaptism was defined not only by belief but by practice, discipline, and the willingness to endure persecution.

The conditions that produced Anabaptism were not unique to Switzerland, nor were they inevitable. They emerged from a convergence of technological change, theological inquiry, and social structures that bound religion to governance. Understanding these origins clarifies why Anabaptism was perceived as uniquely dangerous and why its insistence on voluntary faith carried consequences far beyond doctrinal debate.

In later generations, Mennonites would interpret these early conflicts as foundational to their identity. The emphasis on choice, conscience, and commitment did not arise in abstraction but through confrontation with systems that denied the legitimacy of voluntary belief. The act of choosing the church, first articulated through baptism, became a defining feature of Mennonite history and memory.

Endnotes for Chapter 1

[1] Dyck, Cornelius J. *An Introduction to Mennonite History.* Scottdale, PA: Herald Press, 1993.
[2] Lehmann-Haupt, Hellmut. *Gutenberg and the Master of the Playing Cards.* New Haven, CT: Yale University Press, 1966.
[3] Hostetler, John A. *Amish Society.* 4th ed. Baltimore: Johns Hopkins University Press, 1993.
[4] Smith, C. Henry. *The Story of the Mennonites.* Revised by Cornelius Krahn. Newton, KS: Mennonite Publishing Office, 1950.
[5] Stayer, James M. *Anabaptists and the Sword.* Rev. ed. Lawrence, KS: Coronado Press, 1976. Reprint, Eugene, OR: Wipf & Stock, 2002.

Chapter 2: Infant Baptism and the Meaning of Salvation

The rejection of infant baptism was the most visible and controversial feature of early Anabaptism. Unlike earlier reform disputes, this challenge reached beyond theology to the structure of society itself.

Infant baptism had been widely practiced in Western Christianity since late antiquity. By the medieval period, it was understood as necessary for salvation, removing original sin and incorporating the child into the Christian community. Infant baptism was understood as a theological necessity tied to salvation, original sin, and divine grace. To question infant baptism was therefore to question the moral legitimacy of an entire social order.[1]

The theological justification for infant baptism rested on interpretations of original sin and divine grace. Influenced by Augustine, medieval theologians taught that all humans inherited a sinful nature and required baptism to cleanse them of guilt. Infants, though incapable of conscious wrongdoing, were nonetheless believed to carry the stain of original sin. Baptism ensured their salvation and protected them from eternal punishment should they die young.[2]

By the late fifteenth and early sixteenth centuries, some theologians and lay believers began to reexamine these assumptions. Increased access to scripture encouraged closer reading of New Testament accounts of baptism, which consistently described the rite as following repentance and belief. Anabaptists argued that baptism in the New Testament presupposed understanding and voluntary commitment. They maintained that infants, lacking moral awareness, could not meaningfully participate in the sacrament.[3]

Salvation required repentance, belief, and obedience, none of which could be exercised involuntarily. Anabaptists contended that sin entered human experience through conscious knowledge of good and evil. Because infants had not yet acquired such knowledge, they were not morally accountable in the same way as adults. Baptism, therefore, could not function as a remedy for sin that had not yet been consciously embraced.[4]

For Anabaptists, baptism became the outward sign of an inward transformation rather than a preventative measure against inherited guilt. It marked a decisive break from one's former life and a commitment to follow Christ's teachings. This understanding placed baptism within the broader framework of conversion, emphasizing personal responsibility and ethical conduct. Faith was not assumed at birth but demonstrated through conscious action.

Catholic authorities responded by reaffirming the necessity of infant baptism. Protestant reformers, despite rejecting many Catholic doctrines, largely retained the practice. Martin Luther defended infant baptism by arguing that faith could exist in a hidden or dormant form, even in infants. He compared infant faith to that of sleeping adults, asserting that lack of conscious awareness did not negate genuine belief.

Anabaptists rejected this reasoning as speculative and unsupported by scripture. They insisted that faith must be active and expressed through understanding and obedience. Appeals to hidden faith, they argued, undermined the moral seriousness of Christian commitment and obscured the distinction between belief and conformity. Salvation, in their view, could not be reduced to sacramental participation detached from conscious discipleship.

The rejection of infant baptism carried significant legal consequences. Because baptism functioned as a prerequisite for full participation in civic life, its rejection exposed Anabaptists to legal sanction and social exclusion. Authorities viewed rebaptism not merely as a religious error but as a form of civil disobedience. Laws against Anabaptism reflected this concern, treating religious nonconformity as a threat to public stability.[5]

Anabaptist communities responded by redefining membership and discipline. Admission into the church required instruction, confession of faith, and baptism as an adult. Membership was voluntary but demanding. Those who joined were expected to adhere to strict ethical standards and submit to communal oversight. Baptism thus functioned as both a spiritual and social boundary, separating believers from the surrounding world.

This emphasis on discipline distinguished Anabaptists from other reform movements. Where state churches relied on coercion to enforce conformity, Anabaptist communities depended on internal regulation. Excommunication served as the primary mechanism for maintaining moral integrity. The seriousness with which baptism was treated reinforced the idea that church membership was a deliberate and consequential choice.

The Anabaptist understanding of baptism also reshaped views of childhood and family. Children were regarded as part of the community but not members of the church. They were raised within Anabaptist households and instructed in religious teachings, yet they were expected to make their own decision regarding baptism upon reaching maturity. This approach challenged prevailing assumptions about parental authority and religious inheritance.

Opponents accused Anabaptists of endangering children's souls by withholding baptism. Anabaptists countered that salvation rested in God's mercy rather than sacramental timing. They emphasized divine justice and compassion, arguing that a righteous God would not condemn those incapable of conscious belief. This position further differentiated them from both Catholic and Protestant theologians, who continued to link baptism closely to salvation.[6]

The controversy surrounding infant baptism thus encapsulated broader conflicts over authority, responsibility, and religious identity. It exposed divergent assumptions about the nature of faith and the role of the church in shaping individual lives. For Anabaptists, baptism became the foundational expression of voluntary faith, a visible declaration that belief could not be inherited or enforced.

In later Mennonite tradition, the rejection of infant baptism would remain central to identity formation. It served as a historical marker distinguishing Mennonites from other Christian groups and as a symbolic reminder of the costs associated with choosing belief over conformity. The act of adult baptism embodied the principle that faith must be consciously embraced, even when such a choice carried social and legal consequences.

Endnotes Chapter 2

[1] Dyck, Cornelius J. *An Introduction to Mennonite History.* Scottdale, PA: Herald Press, 1993.
[2] Smith, C. Henry. *The Story of the Mennonites.* Revised by Cornelius Krahn. Newton, KS: Mennonite Publishing Office, 1950.
[3] Estep, William R. *The Anabaptist Story: An Introduction to Sixteenth-Century Anabaptism.* 3rd ed. Grand Rapids, MI: Eerdmans, 1996.
[4] Hostetler, John A. *Amish Society.* 4th ed. Baltimore: Johns Hopkins University Press, 1993.
[5] Stayer, James M. *Anabaptists and the Sword.* Rev. ed. Lawrence, KS: Coronado Press, 1976. Reprint, Eugene, OR: Wipf & Stock, 2002.
[6] Bender, Harold S. Essays on Anabaptist theology and history. Various publications in *Mennonite Quarterly Review*, 1927-1962.

Chapter 3: Zurich and the First Anabaptists

The city of Zurich occupies a central place in the early history of Anabaptism. It was here, within a reforming Protestant context, that disagreements over baptism moved from theological debate to public defiance. The Zurich reform did not initially appear radical. Under the leadership of Ulrich Zwingli, the city sought to align religious practice more closely with scripture while maintaining civic order and unity. This effort reflected a broader pattern across reforming territories, where religious change proceeded under the supervision of municipal authorities.

Zwingli's reform emphasized preaching, biblical study, and the elimination of practices not explicitly supported by scripture. His call for reform attracted a group of younger scholars and laymen who were deeply committed to biblical authority. Among them were Conrad Grebel, Felix Manz, and George Blaurock. These men shared Zwingli's conviction that scripture should guide religious practice, yet they diverged sharply from him on the question of baptism.

As debates intensified, the issue of infant baptism emerged as a point of fracture. Zwingli initially expressed doubts about the practice but hesitated to abandon it. Civic leaders regarded infant baptism as essential to social cohesion and feared that its rejection would undermine legal and communal stability. Faced with pressure from the city council, Zwingli adopted a more cautious position, choosing gradual reform over immediate rupture.[1]

For Grebel and his associates, compromise proved unacceptable. Their reading of the New Testament convinced them that baptism must follow belief and repentance. They concluded that delay or partial reform amounted to disobedience to scripture. This conviction placed them at odds not only with Zwingli but also with the civic authorities who governed religious life in Zurich.

In January 1525, the Zurich council ordered that all infants be baptized within eight days of birth or face exile and prohibited unauthorized preaching. This decree transformed theological disagreement into a legal matter. For dissenters, obedience to the council would require violating their understanding of scripture. The choice before them was stark: submission or separation.

On January 21, 1525, a small group gathered in the home of Felix Manz's mother. There, George Blaurock requested baptism upon confession of faith, and Conrad Grebel baptized him. Blaurock then baptized the others present. This event, often regarded as the first Anabaptist baptism, marked the formal break between the dissenters and the Zurich church.[2]

The significance of this act extended beyond the immediate group. By baptizing one another without clerical authorization, the participants rejected both ecclesiastical hierarchy and civic control over religious practice. Baptism became an act of resistance as well as a declaration of belief. The formation of a voluntary church, separate from state oversight, was no longer theoretical but enacted.

Zurich authorities responded swiftly. Grebel, Manz, and Blaurock were arrested, interrogated, and imprisoned. They were released under orders to cease preaching and abandon adult baptism. When they refused, punishment escalated. Repeated arrests, fines, and periods of confinement followed, reflecting the determination of civic leaders to suppress the movement before it spread further.[3]

Despite persecution, Anabaptist ideas circulated rapidly. Blaurock traveled extensively, preaching and baptizing in rural areas and neighboring territories. His charismatic preaching attracted followers from diverse social backgrounds. Unlike university trained reformers, Blaurock's appeal lay in his direct and passionate delivery. This accessibility alarmed authorities, who feared the spread of dissent among the rural population.

Felix Manz emerged as a key figure in articulating the Anabaptist vision of a free church. He emphasized the separation of church and state and rejected the use of coercion in matters of faith. These positions challenged the prevailing assumption that religious uniformity was necessary for social order. Zurich officials interpreted Manz's refusal to conform as obstinate and dangerous.[4]

In 1527, Zurich authorities imposed the death penalty for rebaptism. Manz was arrested once more, tried, and sentenced to death. On January 5, 1527, he was bound and drowned in the Limmat River. His execution was intended to serve as a public warning to others who might defy the council's authority. For Anabaptists, Manz's death became a powerful symbol of martyrdom.[5]

Conrad Grebel did not live to face execution. Repeated imprisonment weakened his health, and he died of plague in 1526. His early death spared him martyrdom but did not diminish his influence. Grebel's writings and actions continued to shape Anabaptist theology and identity, particularly the emphasis on nonresistance and refusal to swear oaths.

George Blaurock met a violent end in 1529 when he was burned at the stake in Tyrol. His execution reflected the widespread agreement among authorities across confessional lines that Anabaptism posed an unacceptable threat. Catholic and

Protestant rulers alike cooperated in suppressing the movement, underscoring the extent to which Anabaptist beliefs transcended conventional religious divisions.[6]

The Zurich experience established patterns that would recur throughout Anabaptist history. Reformers initially welcomed theological debate but enforced conformity when dissent threatened civic stability. Anabaptists responded by prioritizing obedience to scripture over submission to authority. Persecution, rather than extinguishing the movement, reinforced its identity and clarified its boundaries.

For later Mennonites, the events in Zurich assumed foundational significance. The first adult baptisms, the refusal to compromise, and the willingness to suffer punishment were remembered as defining moments in the formation of a voluntary church. Zurich represented both the promise of reform and the limits imposed by state control. It was here that the principle of choosing the church was enacted with lasting consequences.

Endnotes for Chapter 3

[1] Dyck, Cornelius J. *An Introduction to Mennonite History.* Scottdale, PA: Herald Press, 1993.

[2] Estep, William R. *The Anabaptist Story: An Introduction to Sixteenth-Century Anabaptism.* 3rd ed. Grand Rapids, MI: Eerdmans, 1996.

[3] Smith, C. Henry. *The Story of the Mennonites.* Revised by Cornelius Krahn. Newton, KS: Mennonite Publishing Office, 1950.

[4] Wenger, John C. *Glimpses of Mennonite History and Doctrine.* 2nd ed. Scottdale, PA: Herald Press, 1947.

[5] Stayer, James M. *Anabaptists and the Sword.* Rev. ed. Lawrence, KS: Coronado Press, 1976. Reprint, Eugene, OR: Wipf & Stock, 2002.

[6] Bender, Harold S. Essays on Anabaptist theology and history. Various publications in *Mennonite Quarterly Review*, 1927-1962.

Chapter 4: Martyrdom as Proof of Faith

Persecution was not incidental to the development of early Anabaptism. It was structural. From its inception, the movement confronted legal systems designed to enforce religious conformity and civic obedience. The persistence of Anabaptist belief in the face of systematic repression transformed suffering into a defining element of identity and shaped the theological and communal contours of what would later become Mennonite tradition.

In early modern Europe, religious dissent was treated as a public crime rather than a private conviction. Laws regulating baptism, preaching, and church attendance functioned as mechanisms of social control. Authorities viewed deviation from established religious practice as a threat to order, not merely an error in belief. As a result, Anabaptists were prosecuted under a range of charges that included heresy, sedition, and refusal to obey lawful authority.[1]

The legal framework for persecution varied by territory but shared common features. Imperial mandates outlawed rebaptism and authorized severe penalties, including death. Local ordinances reinforced these measures by criminalizing unauthorized gatherings and preaching. Enforcement was often carried out by both ecclesiastical courts and civic magistrates, reflecting the close alliance between church and state.[2]

Executions were intended to deter dissent and restore conformity. Public punishments served as warnings, demonstrating the consequences of religious noncompliance. Methods of execution differed by region and gender. Men were often executed by drowning, burning, or beheading, while women were more frequently drowned, a practice justified as less brutal but equally final. These distinctions underscored the extent to which punishment was shaped by social norms as well as legal codes.[3]

For Anabaptists, martyrdom came to signify fidelity rather than failure. Those who endured imprisonment, torture, and execution were remembered not as criminals but as witnesses to truth. Accounts of their deaths circulated within Anabaptist communities, reinforcing commitment and offering models of faithfulness under pressure. The willingness to suffer without resistance distinguished Anabaptists from other dissenting groups and contributed to their reputation.

Nonresistance played a central role in shaping Anabaptist responses to persecution. Many Anabaptists interpreted the teachings of Jesus as prohibiting the use of violence under any circumstances. They refused to defend themselves physically, declined military service, and accepted punishment without retaliation. This posture confounded authorities who expected resistance as confirmation of guilt. Instead, passive endurance challenged the moral legitimacy of coercive power.[4]

Martyr narratives emphasized obedience to God over obedience to human authority. Testimonies recorded before execution often highlighted the individual's conscious choice to remain faithful despite the consequences. These narratives framed persecution as a test of sincerity, reinforcing the belief that true faith required sacrifice. In this way, martyrdom functioned as both a theological affirmation and a communal boundary, distinguishing committed believers from those unwilling to endure suffering.

The accumulation of martyr stories contributed to a shared historical memory that extended beyond individual communities. Although Anabaptist groups were geographically dispersed and often isolated from one another, accounts of persecution circulated through letters, oral reports, and later compilations. These shared narratives fostered a sense of collective identity rooted in suffering and endurance rather than institutional continuity.[5]

At the same time, persecution exposed internal tensions within the movement. Not all who sympathized with Anabaptist beliefs were willing to face execution. Some recanted under pressure, while others fled to regions offering greater tolerance. These responses prompted debates over discipline, forgiveness, and the criteria for belonging. The experience of persecution thus accelerated the development of communal norms and mechanisms for regulating membership.

Authorities interpreted Anabaptist steadfastness as obstinacy. Rather than recognizing conscience-driven conviction, officials often viewed refusal to recant as defiance. This perception justified escalating punishment and reinforced the association of Anabaptism with social disorder. Ironically, the severity of repression confirmed Anabaptist claims that the true church could not rely on state power without compromising its integrity.

By the late 1520s and early 1530s, persecution had significantly reduced the number of visible Anabaptist leaders in many regions. Yet the movement persisted through informal networks and underground gatherings. The experience of repression forced Anabaptists to adapt, emphasizing secrecy, mutual support, and internal discipline. These adaptations laid the groundwork for more stable forms of organization in subsequent decades.

For later Mennonites, martyrdom assumed a central place in historical consciousness. The memory of those who suffered and died for their beliefs was preserved as evidence of the costs associated with choosing the church over conformity. Martyrdom narratives were not merely commemorative but instructional, offering moral guidance and reinforcing the principle that faith required deliberate and sustained commitment.

The legacy of persecution shaped Mennonite attitudes toward authority, violence, and community boundaries. The refusal to compel belief through force became a defining characteristic, rooted in the historical experience of being subjected to coercion. In this way, martyrdom was not only a consequence of Anabaptist belief but a formative influence on Mennonite identity.

Endnotes for Chapter 4

[1] Stayer, James M. *Anabaptists and the Sword.* Rev. ed. Lawrence, KS: Coronado Press, 1976. Reprint, Eugene, OR: Wipf & Stock, 2002.
[2] Dyck, Cornelius J. *An Introduction to Mennonite History.* Scottdale, PA: Herald Press, 1993.
[3] Smith, C. Henry. *The Story of the Mennonites.* Revised by Cornelius Krahn. Newton, KS: Mennonite Publishing Office, 1950.
[4] Wenger, John C. *Glimpses of Mennonite History and Doctrine.* 2nd ed. Scottdale, PA: Herald Press, 1947.
[5] Bender, Harold S. Essays on Anabaptist theology and history. Various publications in *Mennonite Quarterly Review*, 1927-1962.

Chapter 5: Münster and the Limits of Reform

The Münster uprising of the early 1530s stands as one of the most consequential crises in Anabaptist history. Although the movement that took control of the city differed significantly from peaceful Anabaptist groups, its actions had lasting implications for all who rejected infant baptism and state churches. Münster became a defining moment that reshaped public perception, intensified persecution, and forced Anabaptists to clarify the boundaries of belief and practice.

Münster was a prosperous city in Westphalia, a region of the Holy Roman Empire in which weak centralized authority and contested religious leadership created space for radical reform movements. In the early 1530s, tensions between Catholic authorities, Protestant reformers, and civic leaders created an unstable political environment. Into this context arrived itinerant preachers influenced by Anabaptist ideas, including adult baptism and the restoration of a true Christian community. These ideas resonated with segments of the population already dissatisfied with ecclesiastical authority.[1]

Under the leadership of Jan Matthijs, a baker from Haarlem, a center of early Reformation activity in the northern Netherlands, the movement in Münster took on an apocalyptic character. Matthijs proclaimed Münster to be the New Jerusalem and predicted the imminent return of Christ. His followers believed they were living at the end of history and that God had chosen the city as the site of final redemption. Adult baptism became compulsory, and those who refused were expelled.[2]

This development marked a decisive departure from earlier Anabaptist emphasis on voluntary faith. Where peaceful Anabaptists insisted on persuasion and personal conviction, the

Münster leaders enforced conformity within the city. The transformation of Münster into a theocratic community combined religious zeal with political control, reinforcing fears that Anabaptism inherently led to disorder and violence.

The bishop of Münster, who had been forced into exile, assembled an army with support from regional princes and laid siege to the city in 1534. The siege lasted over a year and subjected the inhabitants to severe deprivation. As conditions worsened, leadership passed to Jan van Leiden following the death of Matthijs during a failed sortie. Van Leiden intensified the radical program, declaring himself king and introducing polygamy, which he justified through selective biblical interpretation.[3]

These measures further alienated both supporters and observers. While some inhabitants accepted the new order as divinely mandated, others attempted to flee the city and were executed by the leadership. The combination of religious absolutism and coercion deepened internal divisions and contributed to the eventual collapse of the movement.

In June 1535, Münster fell to the besieging forces. The city was retaken through military assault, and the population was subjected to widespread violence. Leaders of the movement were captured rather than immediately executed. After prolonged imprisonment and public display, they were tortured and killed. Their bodies were placed in iron cages and suspended from the tower of St. Lambert's Church as a warning to others who might challenge established authority.

The aftermath of Münster reverberated throughout Europe. Authorities cited the episode as proof that Anabaptism was inherently dangerous and subversive. Laws against rebaptism were enforced more rigorously, and persecution intensified even against groups that explicitly rejected violence and political ambition. The distinction between peaceful Anabaptists and radical movements was largely ignored by opponents.

For Anabaptists who survived, Münster became a point of reckoning. The association of Anabaptism with apocalyptic violence threatened the survival of all nonconforming groups. Leaders who advocated nonresistance and voluntary faith were compelled to articulate clear theological and practical boundaries. The rejection of coercion, communal ownership enforced by force, and apocalyptic militancy became central to efforts at reform within the movement.

Menno Simons emerged in the immediate aftermath of Münster as a figure who explicitly addressed the crisis. He condemned the violence and excesses of the Münster leaders and sought to reclaim Anabaptism from association with rebellion. His writings emphasized discipleship, humility, and obedience to Christ's teachings rather than eschatological speculation or political control. In doing so, he provided a framework through which peaceful Anabaptist communities could distance themselves from the Münster legacy.[4]

The memory of Münster continued to shape Anabaptist identity long after the city's collapse. For opponents, it served as justification for continued repression. For Mennonites, it functioned as a cautionary narrative illustrating the dangers of conflating religious conviction with coercive power. The episode reinforced the belief that the true church must remain separate from state authority and resist the temptation to enforce belief through force.

Münster thus represents the limits of reform within the Anabaptist tradition. It exposed the vulnerabilities inherent in radical interpretations of scripture divorced from communal accountability and ethical restraint. At the same time, it clarified the principles that would come to define Mennonite identity. Voluntary faith, nonresistance, and discipline emerged not only as theological commitments but as practical safeguards against the excesses that Münster exemplified.

Endnotes for Chapter 5

[1] Dyck, Cornelius J. *An Introduction to Mennonite History.* Scottdale, PA: Herald Press, 1993.
[2] Smith, C. Henry. *The Story of the Mennonites.* Revised by Cornelius Krahn. Newton, KS: Mennonite Publishing Office, 1950.
[3] Stayer, James M. *Anabaptists and the Sword.* Rev. ed. Lawrence, KS: Coronado Press, 1976. Reprint, Eugene, OR: Wipf & Stock, 2002.
[4] Simons, Menno. *The Complete Writings of Menno Simons.* English translations of sixteenth-century works. Accessed January 2000.

Chapter 6: From Priest to Anabaptist Leader

In the aftermath of Münster and intensified persecution, Menno Simons emerged as a stabilizing figure among peaceful Anabaptist communities. The collapse of the Münster experiment had intensified persecution and discredited Anabaptism in the eyes of both authorities and the public. Peaceful Anabaptist groups faced the dual challenge of survival and redefinition. It was within this context that Simons emerged not as the originator of new doctrines but as a stabilizing figure who provided coherence, discipline, and continuity to scattered communities.

Born in Friesland in 1496, Menno Simons was ordained as a Catholic priest in 1524. By his own account, he entered the priesthood with limited theological preparation and relied heavily on established church teaching rather than personal study of scripture. His doubts began quietly. During the celebration of the mass, Simons questioned the doctrine of transubstantiation, the belief that the bread and wine became the literal body and blood of Christ. Troubled by this uncertainty, he turned to the New Testament in search of clarity.[1]

This initial questioning led to broader examination of church practices. Simons became aware of debates surrounding baptism after the execution of an Anabaptist in nearby Leeuwarden. Disturbed by the severity of the punishment, he began to study the scriptural basis for infant baptism. His investigation convinced him that the practice lacked clear biblical support. Unlike reformers who framed infant baptism as a matter of tradition or covenant theology, Simons concluded that baptism required conscious belief and repentance.[2]

For several years, Simons remained within the Catholic Church while privately grappling with these conclusions. He was reluctant to abandon his position, aware of the personal risk and social consequences such a decision entailed. His hesitation reflected the broader dilemma faced by many clergy during the Reformation, who balanced growing theological doubts against institutional loyalty and personal security.

The turning point came in 1536, when Simons publicly renounced his priesthood. In a written declaration, he described his decision as compelled by conscience and fear of divine judgment rather than political calculation. He rejected the comforts and protections of clerical life in favor of an uncertain existence marked by exile and danger. This renunciation signaled his full break with the Catholic Church and his alignment with Anabaptist belief.[3]

Following his departure, Simons went into hiding and spent an extended period studying scripture. During this time, he came into contact with peaceful Anabaptist groups who rejected the violence associated with Münster. He was baptized as an adult by Obbe Philips, a former Anabaptist leader who had become disillusioned by internal divisions and extremism. Philips soon withdrew from active leadership, leaving a vacuum that Simons would gradually fill.[4]

Simons did not seek prominence. His leadership developed through necessity rather than ambition. Anabaptist communities across the Netherlands and northern Germany were fragmented and vulnerable. Without centralized organization or formal clergy, they depended on itinerant leaders for instruction, discipline, and pastoral care. Simons assumed this role, traveling extensively under constant threat of arrest and execution.

His contribution lay in systematizing belief and practice. Simons emphasized a disciplined church composed of committed believers who voluntarily submitted to communal oversight. He rejected apocalyptic speculation and political involvement, insisting that the church's mission was spiritual rather than civic. Nonresistance, humility, and ethical conduct formed the core of his teaching.[5]

Simons also addressed the issue of authority within the church. Rejecting hierarchical structures, he nevertheless argued for orderly leadership grounded in moral integrity and scriptural knowledge. Ministers were to serve the community rather than dominate it. Discipline, including excommunication when necessary, was presented as a means of preserving the church's integrity rather than exercising control.

Throughout his writings, Simons distinguished sharply between true discipleship and nominal Christianity. He criticized state churches for relying on coercion and sacramental participation rather than genuine belief. At the same time, he warned Anabaptists against fanaticism and disorder, stressing obedience, patience, and consistency. This balance appealed to communities seeking stability after years of upheaval.

Authorities regarded Simons as particularly dangerous precisely because of his moderation. His rejection of violence did not translate into acceptance of state authority over religious life. He continued to insist on the separation of church and state and refused to swear oaths or participate in civic governance. These positions ensured that he remained a target of persecution throughout his life.[6]

Despite this pressure, Simons succeeded in fostering a sense of collective identity among dispersed Anabaptist groups. Over time, followers began referring to themselves as Mennonites, not as a declaration of loyalty to an individual but as a means of distinguishing their disciplined, nonviolent approach from other Anabaptist factions. The name signaled continuity, coherence, and commitment to a particular understanding of voluntary faith.

Simons died in 1561 after decades of itinerant leadership. He left no centralized institution but bequeathed a framework of belief and practice that enabled Mennonite communities to endure. His influence lay not in innovation but in consolidation. By clarifying boundaries, rejecting extremism, and emphasizing voluntary commitment, Simons helped transform a persecuted movement into a recognizable religious tradition.

Endnotes for Chapter 6

[1] Simons, Menno. *The Complete Writings of Menno Simons.* English translations of sixteenth-century works. Accessed January 2000.
[2] Smith, C. Henry. *The Story of the Mennonites.* Revised by Cornelius Krahn. Newton, KS: Mennonite Publishing Office, 1950.
[3] Bender, Harold S. Essays on Anabaptist theology and history. Various publications in *Mennonite Quarterly Review*, 1927-1962.
[4] Dyck, Cornelius J. *An Introduction to Mennonite History.* Scottdale, PA: Herald Press, 1993.
[5] Wenger, John C. *Glimpses of Mennonite History and Doctrine.* 2nd ed. Scottdale, PA: Herald Press, 1947.
[6] Stayer, James M. *Anabaptists and the Sword.* Rev. ed. Lawrence, KS: Coronado Press, 1976. Reprint, Eugene, OR: Wipf & Stock, 2002.

Chapter 7: Voluntary Faith and the Separation of Church and State

The Anabaptist insistence on voluntary faith had unavoidable political consequences. In early modern Europe, church and state were closely intertwined, and religious conformity functioned as a tool of governance. To separate faith from coercion was therefore not only a theological claim but a challenge to established social structures.

In most European territories, citizenship and religious affiliation were inseparable. Individuals were born into both a political jurisdiction and a church. Participation in religious rites, including baptism, communion, and attendance at worship, was mandated by law. These practices reinforced communal unity and enabled authorities to monitor moral behavior. Dissent threatened not only doctrinal uniformity but the mechanisms through which communities maintained order.[1]

Mennonites rejected the premise that faith could be compelled. Drawing on New Testament teachings, they argued that belief required personal conviction and obedience rather than external enforcement. Conversion was understood as an inward transformation manifested through ethical conduct and public confession. This understanding rendered coercive religion ineffective and illegitimate.

The concept of a voluntary church followed logically from this position. Membership was not automatic but contingent upon instruction, repentance, and adult baptism. Individuals chose to join the church and accepted the responsibilities that accompanied that choice. Discipline was internal and communal rather than imposed by civil authorities. In this model, the church existed independently of the state and derived its authority from shared commitment rather than legal mandate.

This separation had practical implications. Mennonites refused to swear oaths, citing biblical injunctions against invoking God to guarantee human promises. Oaths were central to legal systems, used to secure testimony, loyalty, and contracts. Refusal to swear oaths placed Mennonites at odds with courts and civic institutions and reinforced perceptions of disloyalty.[2]

Military service presented another point of conflict. Mennonites interpreted Christ's teachings as prohibiting violence, even in defense of the state. They declined to bear arms, serve in militias, or participate in warfare. While some territories permitted exemptions in exchange for fines or alternative service, others regarded refusal as treasonous. Nonresistance thus carried significant social and legal consequences.

Mennonite views on governance were often misunderstood. Their refusal to participate in civic offices did not reflect indifference to social order. Rather, they distinguished between the purposes of church and state. The state was understood as an institution established to maintain law and order through force when necessary. The church, by contrast, was tasked with spiritual care, moral guidance, and the cultivation of faith without coercion.[3]

This distinction allowed Mennonites to acknowledge the legitimacy of secular authority while limiting its reach. They obeyed civil laws insofar as those laws did not conflict with religious conviction. When conflicts arose, obedience to God took precedence. This position placed Mennonites in a precarious position, as authorities interpreted selective obedience as subversion.

Internal discipline became essential to maintaining the integrity of a voluntary church. Because Mennonites rejected external enforcement, they relied on communal accountability to regulate behavior. Members were expected to adhere to ethical standards that reflected their commitment to Christ's teachings. Failure to do so could result in admonition, suspension from communion, or excommunication.

Excommunication served both corrective and symbolic functions. It reinforced the seriousness of church membership and signaled the boundaries of the community. At the same time, it underscored the voluntary nature of belonging. Individuals could leave the church, but remaining required adherence to shared norms. This balance between freedom and discipline distinguished Mennonite communities from both state churches and more radical movements.

The separation of church and state also shaped Mennonite attitudes toward wealth, social status, and power. Accumulation of authority within the church was viewed with suspicion, as it risked replicating the hierarchical structures Mennonites had rejected. Leaders were expected to serve rather than govern, and decisions were often made collectively. This emphasis on humility and mutual responsibility reinforced communal cohesion.

Over time, Mennonite commitment to voluntary faith and separation from the state became defining features of identity. These principles were not abstract ideals but practical responses to historical experience. Persecution, exclusion, and marginalization reinforced the conviction that faith imposed by force undermined its own purpose.

For later generations, the memory of these conflicts informed attitudes toward authority and participation in broader society.

While Mennonite communities adapted to changing political contexts, the foundational belief that faith must be chosen rather than inherited remained central. The separation of church and state, first articulated as a necessity for survival, became a core element of Mennonite self understanding.

Endnotes for Chapter 7

[1] Dyck, Cornelius J. *An Introduction to Mennonite History.* Scottdale, PA: Herald Press, 1993.
[2] Hostetler, John A. *Amish Society.* 4th ed. Baltimore: Johns Hopkins University Press, 1993.
[3] Bender, Harold S. Essays on Anabaptist theology and history. Various publications in *Mennonite Quarterly Review*, 1927-1962.

Chapter 8: Nonresistance and Survival

Nonresistance was one of the most distinctive and consequential features of Mennonite belief. Rooted in Anabaptist interpretations of the New Testament, it shaped how Mennonites responded to persecution, interacted with the state, and understood their place in society. Rather than functioning as an abstract moral principle, nonresistance developed as a practical strategy for survival within hostile political environments.

Early Anabaptists drew heavily on the teachings of Jesus, particularly passages that emphasized love of enemies, refusal of retaliation, and submission to suffering. These teachings were interpreted as binding ethical commands rather than aspirational ideals. Violence, even in self defense or defense of the innocent, was viewed as incompatible with Christian discipleship. This position extended beyond warfare to include legal retaliation, participation in punitive systems, and the use of coercive force in religious matters.[1]

Nonresistance distinguished Mennonites from both Catholic and Protestant contemporaries. While reformers debated the legitimacy of violence in defense of true religion or civil order, Mennonites rejected such reasoning entirely. They maintained that the use of force corrupted the church's witness and compromised obedience to Christ. This stance placed them outside the moral consensus of early modern Europe, where violence was widely accepted as a necessary instrument of governance.

The consequences were immediate and severe. Mennonites refused military service, declined to bear arms, and rejected participation in militias. In times of war, these refusals were interpreted as disloyalty or cowardice. Some territories permitted exemptions in exchange for fines or alternative labor, but others imposed imprisonment, confiscation of property, or expulsion. Nonresistance thus carried tangible economic and social costs.[2]

Nonresistance shaped not only responses to persecution but expectations for daily conduct. Members were expected to endure punishment without retaliation or protest. Martyr narratives emphasized patience, humility, and forgiveness rather than resistance. This posture reinforced communal identity and provided moral coherence in the face of suffering. It also frustrated authorities, who often interpreted passive endurance as obstinate defiance.

Nonresistance required careful negotiation of daily life. Mennonites sought to avoid situations that would compel participation in violence or coercion. This avoidance shaped patterns of settlement, occupation, and migration. Many Mennonites gravitated toward rural areas where they could farm, live communally, and minimize interaction with state institutions. Isolation was not pursued for its own sake but as a means of preserving religious integrity.

The refusal to participate in violence extended to internal community life. Mennonites rejected corporal punishment as a disciplinary tool within the church. Correction was to be administered through admonition, exclusion, and reconciliation rather than force. This approach reinforced the voluntary nature of membership and underscored the belief that moral change could not be compelled.

Nonresistance also informed Mennonite attitudes toward justice and legal redress. Members were encouraged to resolve disputes internally rather than through courts. Litigation was viewed as a form of coercion that undermined communal harmony and reliance on Christian principles. While this practice reduced exposure to external authority, it also required robust internal mechanisms for conflict resolution.[3]

Over time, Mennonite commitment to nonresistance became a defining marker of identity. It distinguished Mennonites from other Anabaptist groups that adopted more militant positions and from Protestant churches that aligned with state power. The principle was transmitted across generations through teaching, discipline, and historical memory. Children were raised on stories that emphasized endurance, sacrifice, and faithfulness under pressure.

Adaptation was nevertheless necessary. As Mennonites migrated to regions offering greater tolerance, including parts of Eastern Europe and later North America, they encountered political systems that accommodated religious diversity to varying degrees. Nonresistance continued to shape relations with the state, but its expression evolved in response to new contexts. Exemptions from military service, negotiated compromises, and alternative forms of civic contribution became part of Mennonite experience.

These adaptations did not eliminate tension. Debates persisted within Mennonite communities over the limits of nonresistance and the extent to which accommodation constituted compromise. Such debates reflected broader challenges inherent in sustaining a voluntary faith tradition within changing political landscapes.

Nonresistance functioned not only as a moral commitment but as a mechanism of survival. It enabled Mennonites to maintain continuity in the absence of political power and institutional protection. By rejecting violence and coercion, Mennonites defined themselves in opposition to dominant modes of authority. This self definition carried costs, but it also provided a framework through which communities could endure persecution, migration, and marginalization.

In the formation of Mennonite identity, nonresistance became inseparable from the act of choosing the church. It embodied the conviction that faith required obedience even when obedience entailed vulnerability. Through nonresistance, Mennonites articulated a vision of religious life grounded in conscience rather than force, a vision shaped by historical necessity and sustained through collective memory.

Endnotes for Chapter 8

[1] Bender, Harold S. Essays on Anabaptist theology and history. Various publications in *Mennonite Quarterly Review*, 1927-1962.
[2] Stayer, James M. *Anabaptists and the Sword.* Rev. ed. Lawrence, KS: Coronado Press, 1976. Reprint, Eugene, OR: Wipf & Stock, 2002.
[3] Wenger, John C. *Glimpses of Mennonite History and Doctrine.* 2nd ed. Scottdale, PA: Herald Press, 1947.

Chapter 9: Worship, Symbols, and Daily Practice

Mennonite worship and daily religious practice developed within the constraints imposed by persecution, separation from the state, and commitment to voluntary faith. These conditions shaped not only what Mennonites believed but how belief was expressed in communal life. Worship practices emphasized simplicity, order, and participation rather than spectacle or sacramental mediation.

Early Mennonite worship took place in private homes, barns, and secluded outdoor locations rather than formal church buildings. The absence of dedicated meetinghouses reflected both necessity and conviction. Public worship exposed congregations to surveillance and punishment, while elaborate structures risked replicating the institutional authority Mennonites had rejected. Over time, meetinghouses emerged, but they remained architecturally plain and functionally oriented.[1]

Worship services centered on preaching, scripture reading, prayer, and communal singing. The sermon occupied a central position, serving as the primary means of instruction and moral guidance. Preaching emphasized ethical conduct, discipleship, and obedience to Christ's teachings rather than doctrinal speculation. Ministers were selected from within the community and were expected to model humility and integrity rather than formal theological training.

Music played a restrained role in worship. Congregational singing was common, but instrumental accompaniment was often avoided. This preference reflected concerns that instruments might distract from spiritual focus or introduce elements of display inconsistent with Mennonite values. Hymns were typically sung slowly and in unison, reinforcing communal participation and equality among worshippers.[2]

Mennonite worship also emphasized silence and reflection. Periods of quiet were incorporated into services, allowing individuals to contemplate scripture and examine their conduct. Emotional expression was generally subdued. Excessive displays of enthusiasm were viewed with suspicion, associated with instability or fanaticism. Order and restraint were considered safeguards against disorder and coercion.

Symbols occupied an important but carefully circumscribed role in Mennonite religious life. Practices such as baptism, communion, and foot washing were retained but interpreted symbolically rather than sacramentally. These rites were understood as outward expressions of inward commitment rather than channels of divine grace.

Adult baptism marked entry into the church and signified a conscious decision to follow Christ. The ritual itself varied by region, including pouring, sprinkling, or immersion. Regardless of form, baptism was preceded by instruction and confession of faith. Its significance lay in the public affirmation of belief and acceptance of communal discipline.[3]

Communion served as a commemorative act rather than a sacramental transformation. Bread and wine symbolized Christ's body and blood and provided an opportunity for self examination and reconciliation. Participation was restricted to baptized members in good standing. The emphasis on preparation reinforced the seriousness of membership and the moral responsibilities associated with belonging.

Foot washing, drawn from the Gospel account of Jesus washing his disciples' feet, functioned as a symbol of humility and mutual service. Congregants washed one another's feet as an expression of equality and submission. This practice underscored the rejection of hierarchy within the church and reinforced communal bonds.

Daily religious practice extended beyond formal worship. Mennonite life was structured around regular devotions, scripture reading, and ethical discipline. Religious instruction occurred within households as well as congregations. Parents bore responsibility for teaching children biblical narratives and moral expectations, preparing them for eventual decision making regarding baptism.

Work and faith were closely linked. Farming and manual labor were not merely economic activities but expressions of stewardship and obedience. Simplicity in lifestyle reflected a commitment to avoiding excess and dependency on wealth. Occupational choices were influenced by the desire to maintain integrity and minimize entanglement with state authority.[4]

Community regulation played a central role in sustaining religious practice. Members were expected to hold one another accountable through admonition and example. Gossip and coercion were discouraged, while correction was framed as an act of care rather than punishment. This approach reinforced the voluntary nature of belonging while maintaining communal standards.

Over time, worship practices varied among Mennonite groups in response to migration, cultural context, and internal division. Some communities adopted more formalized structures, while others retained simpler forms. Despite these differences, core features remained consistent. Worship emphasized participation over performance, symbols over sacraments, and discipline over coercion.

For Mennonites, worship and daily practice embodied the principles articulated in earlier generations. The rejection of imposed belief found expression in communal rituals that required consent and commitment. Simplicity, restraint, and mutual accountability functioned as practical extensions of the conviction that faith must be chosen rather than inherited.

These practices reinforced Mennonite identity not through doctrinal enforcement but through repeated participation in shared forms of life. Worship became a space where historical memory, ethical expectation, and personal conviction converged. In this way, daily religious practice sustained the tradition formed through earlier conflict and adaptation.

Endnotes for Chapter 9

[1] Dyck, Cornelius J. *An Introduction to Mennonite History.* Scottdale, PA: Herald Press, 1993.
[2] Hostetler, John A. *Amish Society.* 4th ed. Baltimore: Johns Hopkins University Press, 1993.
[3] Smith, C. Henry. *The Story of the Mennonites.* Revised by Cornelius Krahn. Newton, KS: Mennonite Publishing Office, 1950.
[4] Bender, Harold S. Essays on Anabaptist theology and history. Various publications in *Mennonite Quarterly Review*, 1927-1962.

Chapter 10: Gender, Dress, and Authority

Gender and dress became among the most visible mechanisms through which Mennonite communities translated theological conviction into everyday discipline. While theological commitments shaped belief and worship, outward practices communicated belonging to both insiders and outsiders. Plain dress and gender differentiation functioned as mechanisms of social regulation within Mennonite communities.

Early Mennonite communities rejected ornate and fashionable clothing, associating display with pride, vanity, and distraction from spiritual life. This rejection was not primarily aesthetic but ethical. Clothing that drew attention to the individual was viewed as incompatible with humility and submission to communal authority. Over time, these convictions developed into formal dress codes that prescribed acceptable styles, colors, and materials.[1]

Gender differentiation was integral to Mennonite understandings of order and authority. Distinct clothing for men and women reinforced assumptions about gender roles rooted in scriptural interpretation. Men and women were assigned complementary responsibilities within the household and the church. These distinctions were understood as divinely ordained rather than socially constructed, reflecting broader early modern assumptions about hierarchy and order.[2]

Women's dress was subject to detailed regulation and carried heightened symbolic significance. Head coverings and modest garments were interpreted as outward signs of obedience and order, grounded in scriptural readings concerning gender hierarchy. These practices functioned as visible commitments to communal discipline, though women's experiences of and responses to these expectations varied across time, place, and community. Compliance signaled belonging, while deviation prompted pastoral concern rather than immediate sanction.[3]

The veil also functioned as a communal identifier. Its presence signaled membership and obedience, while its absence could provoke concern or censure. In this way, dress became a form of discipline, reinforcing expectations without direct coercion. Compliance demonstrated commitment, while deviation prompted communal response.

Men's dress was regulated as well, though with less symbolic emphasis. Plain coats, broadfall trousers, and unadorned hats reflected expectations of humility and restraint. Short hair for men contrasted with long hair for women, reinforcing gender differentiation. Jewelry, including wedding rings, was often prohibited for both sexes as an expression of simplicity and resistance to material display.

Authority within Mennonite communities was gendered. Leadership roles within the church were reserved for men, who served as ministers, elders, and deacons. Women's participation was largely confined to domestic and supportive roles, including childrearing, hospitality, and informal instruction. These arrangements reflected prevailing early modern assumptions about order and authority, reinforced through selective theological interpretation.[4]

Despite these limitations, women played a significant role in sustaining Mennonite communities. Their responsibility for transmitting values within the household positioned them as primary agents of cultural continuity. Women preserved language, customs, and religious instruction, particularly in contexts of migration and displacement. Memoirs and diaries often reveal women's perspectives on faith, discipline, and identity, even when formal authority was denied.

> "They say that the Prussians were surprised that we Germans in Russia had remained so German... What are we but Germans?"[5]

Dress regulations were enforced through communal mechanisms rather than legal sanction. Admonition, counseling, and, in extreme cases, excommunication served to maintain conformity. Because membership was voluntary, continued participation required acceptance of these expectations. This framework allowed Mennonite communities to preserve distinctiveness without relying on external enforcement.

Over time, dress practices evolved in response to migration, economic change, and internal debate. Some Mennonite groups adopted more flexible standards, reserving traditional dress for worship or ceremonial occasions. Others maintained strict adherence as a marker of faithfulness. These variations reflected ongoing negotiation between continuity and adaptation.

Gender roles and dress thus functioned as practical expressions of Mennonite values rather than mere cultural artifacts. They embodied commitments to humility, order, and separation from the world. At the same time, they revealed tensions inherent in sustaining a voluntary religious tradition across changing social contexts.

For Mennonites, visible practices reinforced invisible commitments. Dress and gender differentiation communicated belonging, discipline, and continuity. Through these visible practices, abstract commitments to humility, obedience, and communal accountability were rendered tangible, embedding the act of choosing the church within the routines of daily life.

Endnotes for Chapter 10

[1] Hostetler, John A. *Amish Society.* 4th ed. Baltimore: Johns Hopkins University Press, 1993.
[2] Dyck, Cornelius J. *An Introduction to Mennonite History.* Scottdale, PA: Herald Press, 1993.
[3] Ruth, Merle. *The Significance of the Christian Woman's Veiling.* Scottdale, PA: Herald Press, 1973.
[4] Smith, C. Henry. *The Story of the Mennonites.* Revised by Cornelius Krahn. Newton, KS: Mennonite Publishing Office, 1950.
[5] Anna Baerg, Diary of Anna Baerg: 1916-1924, ed. Gerald Peters (Winnipeg: Canadian Mennonite Bible College Publications, 1985), pg 21.

Chapter 11: Discipline and Community Boundaries

Discipline functioned as a central mechanism through which Mennonite communities maintained coherence, moral accountability, and identity. In the absence of state enforcement and hierarchical authority, internal regulation became essential to sustaining a voluntary church. Discipline allowed a voluntary church to endure without relying on external coercion.

Early Mennonites understood church membership as a serious and binding commitment. Admission through adult baptism signaled acceptance of communal expectations, including ethical conduct, participation in worship, and submission to mutual accountability. Because membership was voluntary, discipline served as the primary means of preserving integrity without resorting to coercion.[1]

Correction followed a graduated process. Minor offenses were addressed through private admonition, consistent with New Testament instruction emphasizing reconciliation and restoration. If an individual persisted in behavior deemed incompatible with church standards, the matter could be brought before the congregation. This progression reflected an effort to balance compassion with responsibility.

Excommunication represented the most severe form of discipline. It involved formal exclusion from communion and, in some cases, social separation. Excommunication was framed as corrective rather than punitive, intended to prompt repentance and eventual restoration. Reentry into the community remained possible, though often difficult and prolonged.[2]

The practice of *Meidung*, or shunning, developed as a means of reinforcing excommunication. Members were instructed to limit social interaction with those who had been excluded, particularly in matters of shared meals and business dealings. The extent of shunning varied by community and period, reflecting ongoing debate over its proper application. Contemporary and later observers differed in their assessment of *Meidung*, debating whether it functioned primarily as moral safeguard or as a source of social harm.

Discipline served both internal and external functions. Internally, it reinforced shared values and clarified expectations. Externally, it distinguished Mennonite communities from surrounding society. The willingness to exclude members who violated communal norms demonstrated that belonging entailed responsibility rather than mere affiliation.

The emphasis on discipline reflected Mennonite experience with persecution and marginalization. Without state protection, communities relied on internal cohesion for survival. Discipline provided a framework for regulating behavior, resolving conflict, and maintaining trust among members. In this context, tolerance of perceived moral deviation threatened not only spiritual integrity but communal stability.[3]

Disciplinary practices also revealed tensions inherent in a voluntary church. The insistence on choice coexisted with strong pressure to conform. While individuals retained the formal freedom to leave the community, continued membership required sustained conformity to communal norms. This dynamic generated ongoing negotiation between personal conscience and collective authority.

Gender and age influenced the application of discipline. Young people approaching baptism were subject to close scrutiny, as their decision carried long term implications. Women, whose behavior was closely tied to family honor and community reputation, often faced stricter regulation in matters of dress and conduct. These patterns reflected broader social norms as well as theological interpretation.

Over time, disciplinary practices evolved in response to migration, legal tolerance, and internal critique. Some Mennonite groups moderated the use of shunning, emphasizing pastoral care and reconciliation. Others retained strict enforcement as a marker of faithfulness. These variations contributed to divisions within the broader Mennonite tradition.

Memoirs and personal narratives frequently reflect the emotional impact of discipline. Accounts of excommunication and shunning reveal experiences of isolation, shame, and spiritual struggle. At the same time, stories of reconciliation underscore the enduring importance of community and belonging. These narratives illustrate how discipline functioned not only as regulation but as a formative experience shaping individual identity.

For Mennonites, community boundaries were neither incidental nor static. They were actively constructed and maintained through discipline, ritual, and memory. Exclusion and inclusion defined the limits of the church and reinforced the seriousness of voluntary commitment.

In the broader formation of Mennonite identity, discipline underscored the cost of choosing the church. Membership entailed accountability that extended beyond belief into every aspect of life. Through discipline, Mennonite communities sought to preserve a form of faith that rejected coercion while demanding accountability, binding belief to responsibility rather than inheritance.

Endnotes for Chapter 11

[1] Dyck, Cornelius J. *An Introduction to Mennonite History.* Scottdale, PA: Herald Press, 1993.

[2] Hostetler, John A. *Amish Society.* 4th ed. Baltimore: Johns Hopkins University Press, 1993.

[3] Bender, Harold S. Essays on Anabaptist theology and history. Various publications in *Mennonite Quarterly Review*, 1927-1962.

Chapter 12: Why Mennonites Divide

Division has been a structural feature of Mennonite history. While often interpreted as evidence of fragmentation or weakness, schism emerged from structural characteristics embedded in the Mennonite tradition itself. Congregational autonomy, geographic dispersion, and divergent interpretations of scripture combined to produce a pattern of division that reflected both conviction and constraint.

From their earliest formation, Mennonite communities lacked a centralized governing authority. Unlike Catholic and Protestant state churches, Mennonites rejected hierarchical structures capable of imposing uniform doctrine or practice across congregations. Authority resided primarily within local communities, which determined standards of belief, discipline, and worship. This autonomy preserved voluntary faith but limited mechanisms for resolving disagreement.[1]

Congregational independence encouraged active engagement with scripture but also intensified interpretive diversity. Without a final arbiter, theological disputes often unfolded through debate and persuasion rather than adjudication. In some cases, prolonged disagreement resulted in the formation of separate congregations. These divisions were not necessarily rooted in hostility but reflected differing convictions regarding faithful practice.

Geographic dispersion further complicated cohesion. Persecution forced Mennonites to migrate frequently, often settling in isolated regions where contact with other communities was limited. Local circumstances shaped religious life, influencing interpretations of scripture and responses to social pressures. Over time, these regional differences solidified into distinct traditions.

Isolation also impeded communication. News traveled slowly, and developments within one community were not always known elsewhere. Practices adopted in response to local conditions could diverge significantly from those of other Mennonite groups. When contact was reestablished, differences that had evolved independently sometimes proved irreconcilable.[2]

Cultural context played a significant role in shaping division. Mennonites adapted to the languages, economies, and legal systems of the regions in which they settled. These adaptations influenced worship practices, education, and attitudes toward authority. While adaptation enabled survival, it also introduced variation that challenged notions of uniform identity.

Disagreements often centered on discipline and boundary maintenance. Questions regarding dress, participation in broader society, and acceptable forms of interaction with non Mennonites generated debate. Some groups favored stricter separation as a safeguard against assimilation, while others pursued accommodation to changing circumstances. These differences reflected contrasting assessments of risk and responsibility rather than doctrinal disagreement.

The absence of centralized authority heightened the stakes of such debates. Decisions reached by one congregation could not bind others. When compromise proved impossible, separation offered a means of preserving conviction without coercion. This pattern aligned with the Mennonite emphasis on voluntary commitment, allowing groups to diverge without imposing conformity.

Division also functioned as a form of adaptation. New congregations emerged in response to migration, generational change, and shifting social conditions. These formations enabled Mennonites to renegotiate identity while retaining core principles. In this sense, division served as a mechanism for continuity rather than dissolution.

Despite separation, shared historical memory maintained a sense of broader affiliation. Stories of persecution, martyrdom, and migration transcended congregational boundaries. These narratives provided a common framework through which diverse groups understood their origins, even as practices diverged.

Critics within and outside the tradition often viewed division as excessive or counterproductive. Mennonites themselves debated the legitimacy of schism, weighing the desire for unity against the imperative of faithfulness. These debates reflected enduring tension between communal cohesion and individual conscience.

In the formation of Mennonite identity, division was not an aberration but a consequence of foundational commitments. The rejection of coercive authority and insistence on voluntary faith limited the capacity for enforced unity. As a result, Mennonite history is characterized by plurality shaped by conviction, context, and choice.

Endnotes for Chapter 12

[1] Dyck, Cornelius J. *An Introduction to Mennonite History.* Scottdale, PA: Herald Press, 1993.
[2] Smith, C. Henry. *The Story of the Mennonites.* Revised by Cornelius Krahn. Newton, KS: Mennonite Publishing Office, 1950.

Chapter 13: Amish, Hutterites, and Mennonite Brethren

The emergence of distinct Mennonite groups illustrates how shared origins produced divergent expressions of faith under varying historical conditions. The Amish, Hutterites, and Mennonite Brethren each developed in response to specific social pressures, theological priorities, and interpretations of communal responsibility. These divisions did not arise from doctrinal rupture alone but from differing assessments of how best to preserve a voluntary and disciplined church.

The Amish originated in the late seventeenth century within Mennonite communities in Switzerland and southern Germany. Jakob Ammann, a Mennonite elder, argued that existing disciplinary practices had become lax and insufficiently enforced. Central to his critique was the application of *Meidung*, or shunning. Ammann maintained that excommunicated members should be subject to strict social avoidance, including exclusion from shared meals and daily interaction.[1]

Ammann's insistence on rigorous discipline reflected concern that accommodation threatened the integrity of the church. He viewed leniency as a failure of accountability that blurred the boundary between the faithful and the world. Opponents argued that Ammann's approach risked excessive severity and undermined reconciliation. When compromise proved impossible, Ammann and his followers separated, forming what became known as the Amish.

Amish communities emphasized separation from broader society through plain dress, limited technology, and rural settlement. These practices were intended to safeguard humility, communal cohesion, and religious discipline. The rejection of modern conveniences functioned not as a rejection of progress per se but as a means of limiting dependence on external systems perceived as corrosive to faith.[2]

The Hutterites emerged earlier, during the mid sixteenth century, under the leadership of Jacob Hutter. Unlike other Anabaptist groups, Hutterites emphasized communal ownership of property as a requirement of Christian faith. Drawing on interpretations of apostolic practice described in the Book of Acts, they argued that true discipleship necessitated the abandonment of private property.[3]

Hutterite communities organized themselves into Bruderhof settlements, where members shared resources, labor, and income. This communal structure distinguished them sharply from other Mennonites, who generally maintained private ownership. Hutterites viewed the economic community as a safeguard against inequality and individualism, while critics questioned its feasibility and scriptural necessity.

The communal lifestyle exposed Hutterites to particular forms of persecution. Their visible separation and perceived wealth attracted hostility from authorities and bandits alike. Despite these challenges, Hutterite communities demonstrated remarkable continuity, preserving language, customs, and communal organization across centuries and migrations.

The Mennonite Brethren emerged much later, in the nineteenth century, within Mennonite communities in the Russian Empire. Influenced by evangelical movements emphasizing personal conversion and revival, some Mennonites criticized what they perceived as spiritual complacency and insufficient discipline within existing congregations. These critics called for renewed emphasis on individual faith experience and moral rigor.[4]

Disagreements centered on issues such as alcohol consumption, church discipline, and the role of personal conversion narratives. When reconciliation failed, dissenting groups formed separate congregations known as Mennonite Brethren. Unlike the Amish and Hutterites, Mennonite Brethren retained many aspects of broader Protestant culture, including missionary activity and structured education.

These three groups illustrate different responses to a shared challenge. Each sought to preserve Mennonite principles of voluntary faith, discipline, and separation from coercive authority, yet each emphasized different mechanisms for achieving that goal. The Amish prioritized strict boundary maintenance, the Hutterites communal ownership, and the Mennonite Brethren personal conversion and revival.

Despite their differences, these groups shared a common historical memory rooted in Anabaptist origins. Narratives of persecution, migration, and commitment continued to shape identity across divisions. While practices diverged, foundational convictions regarding voluntary faith and communal accountability remained central.

The proliferation of Mennonite groups underscores the adaptability of the tradition. Division functioned as a means of resolving conflict without coercion, allowing communities to pursue faithfulness according to conscience. These separations, though often painful, reflected the enduring tension between unity and conviction that has characterized Mennonite history.

In examining these divisions, it becomes clear that Mennonite identity cannot be reduced to a single expression. Rather, it encompasses a range of practices shaped by historical context and interpretive choice. The Amish, Hutterites, and Mennonite Brethren represent distinct pathways through which Mennonites have sought to live out the principle of choosing the church.

Endnotes for Chapter 13

[1] Hostetler, John A. *Amish Society.* 4th ed. Baltimore: Johns Hopkins University Press, 1993.
[2] Dyck, Cornelius J. *An Introduction to Mennonite History.* Scottdale, PA: Herald Press, 1993.
[3] Smith, C. Henry. The Story of the Mennonites. Revised by Cornelius Krahn. Newton, KS: Mennonite Publishing Office, 1950.
[4] Bekker, Jacob P. *Origin of the Mennonite Brethren Church.* Hillsboro, KS: Mennonite Brethren Publishing House, 1973.

Chapter 14: Why Mennonites Write Memoirs

Personal narrative occupies a prominent place in Mennonite historical expression. Memoirs, diaries, interviews, and autobiographical reflections have served as important vehicles for preserving memory, transmitting values, and interpreting identity. These texts do not merely recount individual lives but situate personal experience within a broader communal history shaped by persecution, migration, and faith.

The prevalence of memoir writing among Mennonites reflects the absence of centralized institutions capable of producing official histories. Without a singular ecclesiastical authority to define doctrine or narrative, Mennonite communities relied on personal testimony to convey meaning across generations. Individual stories became repositories of collective memory, linking private experience to shared historical frameworks.[1]

Mennonite memoirs often assume familiarity with communal norms and values. Authors frequently begin their narratives in adulthood, presupposing childhood immersion in Mennonite culture. This narrative choice reflects the assumption that readers share an understanding of religious practice, discipline, and social expectations. When background is provided, it typically situates the author within a specific geographic and cultural community rather than offering comprehensive doctrinal explanation.

Geographic placement serves a crucial function in Mennonite narratives. Authors commonly identify the village, region, or migration route associated with their family. These references anchor personal experience within a network of historical movement and displacement. For Mennonite readers, such details signal communal affiliation and lineage. For outside readers, they provide essential context for understanding the conditions that shaped belief and practice.

Language plays a similar role. References to German dialects, particularly Low German, appear frequently in memoirs and diaries. Language functions as both a marker of continuity and a boundary against assimilation. Even when authors write in English, the inclusion of German phrases underscores the persistence of cultural identity across generations and migrations.

Mennonite memoirs frequently emphasize the interplay between individual conscience and communal expectation. Authors describe growing up within a structured religious environment that provided moral clarity but limited personal autonomy. This tension often forms the narrative core, culminating in a period of questioning, struggle, or crisis that precedes conversion or reaffirmation of faith.

Conversion narratives occupy a central position within Mennonite life writing. Unlike traditions that emphasize dramatic emotional transformation, Mennonite conversion accounts often describe gradual realization, ethical reckoning, or submission to perceived divine calling. The experience is presented not as spontaneous inspiration but as the resolution of prolonged internal conflict.

"While arguing with the Lord, peace evaded us."[2]

These narratives function pedagogically. They model appropriate responses to doubt, temptation, and suffering. Younger readers encounter examples of perseverance, obedience, and humility that reinforce communal values. In this way, memoirs serve as informal instructional texts, complementing formal religious teaching.

Women's narratives are particularly significant. Although excluded from formal leadership roles, women frequently preserved family history through diaries and memoirs. Their writings document domestic life, migration, hardship, and faith practice from perspectives often absent from institutional records. These accounts reveal how religious identity was sustained through everyday labor, caregiving, and moral instruction.[3]

Memoirs also address experiences of discipline and exclusion. Authors recount episodes of admonition, excommunication, and reconciliation, often reflecting on the emotional consequences of communal regulation. These narratives do not uniformly condemn discipline but explore its complexity, acknowledging both its protective and painful dimensions.

Historical trauma functions as a structuring element in Mennonite life writing. Accounts of persecution, war, displacement, and loss recur across generations. These experiences are not treated as isolated tragedies but as formative elements in the construction of collective identity. Suffering is interpreted through theological frameworks that emphasize endurance and faithfulness rather than triumph.

The act of writing itself functions as an assertion of continuity. By recording personal experience, authors affirm their connection to a lineage defined by movement and survival. Memoirs bridge temporal gaps, allowing later generations to engage with the struggles and decisions of their predecessors.

In the context of this study, Mennonite memoirs provide insight into how historical principles are internalized and reinterpreted over time. They reveal how the act of choosing the church is revisited in each generation, shaped by changing circumstances yet anchored in inherited narratives.

Memoirs do not offer a singular Mennonite voice. Rather, they present a range of perspectives that reflect diversity within the tradition. Taken together, they illuminate the processes through which identity is negotiated, preserved, and transformed. Through personal narrative, Mennonites have constructed a history that is both individual and communal, grounded in memory and sustained through storytelling.

Endnotes for Chapter 14

[1] Dyck, Cornelius J. *An Introduction to Mennonite History.* Scottdale, PA: Herald Press, 1993.
[2] Wall, Cornelius and Agnes. As We Remember. Hillsboro, KS: Mennonite Brethren Publishing House, 1979, pg. 42.
[3] Klassen, Pamela E. *Going by the Moon and the Stars: Stories of Two Russian Mennonite Women.* Waterloo, ON: Wilfrid Laurier University Press, 1994.

Chapter 15: Conversion as Crisis

Conversion occupies a central place in Mennonite self understanding. While theological formulations emphasize adult baptism and conscious faith, personal narratives reveal conversion as a process marked by conflict, uncertainty, and moral reckoning. Rather than a single moment of transformation, conversion often emerges as a response to crisis that compels individuals to confront the tension between inherited identity and personal conviction.

Mennonite conversion narratives typically begin within a context of communal belonging. Individuals are raised within a religious culture that provides moral structure, historical memory, and clear expectations. This environment fosters familiarity with belief but does not guarantee commitment. Conversion becomes necessary precisely because faith is not assumed to be automatic or inherited.[1]

Crisis often precipitates conversion. This crisis may take the form of personal loss, moral failure, social dislocation, or confrontation with mortality. In historical narratives, persecution and war frequently serve this function. In more settled contexts, crisis may arise from internal conflict between desire and obligation. Regardless of form, crisis disrupts routine and forces reflection on belief and responsibility.

Mennonite narratives frame crisis as an opportunity for self examination rather than as divine punishment. Authors describe periods of restlessness, doubt, or dissatisfaction that signal the inadequacy of inherited faith. These experiences are interpreted as preparatory, exposing the individual's need for deliberate commitment.

Conversion is portrayed as a response to perceived divine calling rather than emotional impulse. Accounts emphasize deliberation, struggle, and submission. Individuals weigh the consequences of baptism, aware that membership entails discipline and accountability. The decision to join the church thus represents acceptance of constraint as well as belief.

This emphasis distinguishes Mennonite conversion narratives from those in revivalist traditions. Emotional intensity is present but restrained. Dramatic language gives way to reflection on ethical transformation and obedience. Conversion is validated through changed conduct rather than momentary experience.[2]

Conversion narratives frequently involve confrontation with pride. Individuals recount resistance to surrendering autonomy or social standing. Acceptance of baptism requires humility, acknowledgment of dependence, and willingness to submit to communal authority. This aspect of conversion reinforces the Mennonite emphasis on obedience as a marker of sincerity.

Family relationships play a significant role in these narratives. The decision to be baptized may strain familial bonds, particularly when individuals join a different Mennonite group or embrace stricter discipline. Conversion thus becomes a site where personal conscience intersects with communal expectation and loyalty.

Gender influences how conversion is narrated. Men's accounts often emphasize public confession and leadership responsibility, while women's narratives focus on internal struggle, moral clarity, and service. These differences reflect gendered expectations within Mennonite communities rather than divergent spiritual experiences.

Conversion is not presented as the resolution of struggle. Narratives consistently stress that baptism marks the beginning rather than the culmination of faith. The convert enters a life characterized by ongoing discipline, temptation, and accountability. This framing discourages complacency and reinforces the idea that faith requires sustained effort.

> "The struggle was on. The peace of God left us… He was taking us, particularly me, into a special training session to teach me not to speak or act hastily."[3]

The repetition of conversion narratives across generations serves an instructional purpose. They provide models for interpreting doubt, suffering, and moral failure. Younger readers encounter narratives that normalize struggle and emphasize perseverance. Conversion becomes a shared language through which Mennonites articulate identity and continuity.

In historical memoirs, conversion narratives also function as boundary markers. They distinguish those who have consciously chosen the church from those who merely inhabit its culture. This distinction reinforces the voluntary nature of membership and affirms the central premise that faith must be chosen.

Through conversion narratives, Mennonites negotiate the relationship between past and present. Individuals situate their personal decisions within a lineage of belief shaped by persecution, migration, and sacrifice. Conversion becomes a reenactment of historical choice, linking personal experience to collective memory.

In this way, conversion functions as both personal crisis and communal affirmation. It resolves internal conflict while reinforcing shared values. Mennonite identity is sustained not through inherited status but through repeated acts of choosing the church, each shaped by circumstance yet grounded in enduring tradition.

Endnotes for Chapter 15

[1] Bender, Harold S. Essays on Anabaptist theology and history. Various publications in *Mennonite Quarterly Review*, 1927-1962.

[2] Klassen, Pamela E. *Going by the Moon and the Stars: Stories of Two Russian Mennonite Women.* Waterloo, ON: Wilfrid Laurier University Press, 1994.

[3] Cornelius and Agnes Wall, As We Remember (Hillsboro, KS: Mennonite Brethren Publishing House, 1979), 34.

Chapter 16: War, Displacement, and Identity

War and displacement have been recurring forces in Mennonite history, shaping both communal structures and personal identity. While persecution defined the earliest Anabaptist experience, later generations encountered conflict through imperial expansion, revolution, and forced migration. These experiences disrupted established patterns of life and compelled Mennonites to reinterpret faith, belonging, and survival.

Mennonite migration was often reactive rather than aspirational. Communities relocated in response to legal pressure, military conscription, and threats to religious autonomy. Early movements across Europe were followed by larger migrations to Eastern Europe, particularly to regions of present day Poland, Ukraine, and Russia. These territories offered relative tolerance in exchange for agricultural expertise and economic contribution.[1]

Settlement in Eastern Europe enabled Mennonites to establish stable communities while maintaining separation from state churches. Privileges granted by ruling authorities often included exemption from military service, freedom of worship, and local self administration. These arrangements allowed Mennonites to preserve nonresistance and voluntary faith while participating economically in broader society.

This stability proved temporary. Political change repeatedly undermined negotiated protections. The erosion of privileges in the Russian Empire during the nineteenth century forced Mennonites to confront the possibility of compulsory military service. Debates over accommodation and migration intensified, leading many communities to relocate to North America.[2]

The experience of war disrupted Mennonite assumptions about separation and security. World conflicts exposed communities to violence, displacement, and moral ambiguity. Pacifist commitments were tested as Mennonites navigated conscription, alternative service, and accusations of disloyalty. These pressures varied by region and period but consistently challenged the feasibility of nonresistance within modern nation states.

Revolution introduced additional complexity. The Russian Revolution subjected Mennonite communities to violence, famine, and confiscation of property. Churches were closed, religious instruction suppressed, and leaders targeted. For many Mennonites, the revolution represented a rupture that severed continuity with past generations. Displacement became not only physical but cultural and spiritual.[3]

Personal narratives from this period reflect profound disorientation. Authors describe loss of homeland, family separation, and uncertainty regarding survival. Religious identity, previously sustained through stable communal structures, required reinterpretation in exile. Faith was no longer reinforced by routine but tested through instability.

Migration to North America and other regions offered refuge but introduced new challenges. Mennonites encountered societies that permitted religious diversity yet demanded civic participation. Negotiating pacifism, education, and economic integration required adaptation. Communities debated how to preserve identity without replicating isolation that was no longer enforced by law.

War experiences reshaped conversion narratives. For some individuals, exposure to violence intensified commitment to nonresistance. For others, it generated doubt, anger, or reassessment of inherited beliefs. Memoirs recount struggles to reconcile suffering with theological frameworks emphasizing obedience and endurance.

Women's accounts provide particular insight into displacement. Responsible for maintaining family cohesion under extreme conditions, women documented daily survival, moral instruction, and emotional labor. Their narratives reveal how faith was sustained through caregiving, prayer, and memory when institutional structures collapsed.[4]

Displacement also altered the transmission of historical memory. In new environments, Mennonite identity relied increasingly on storytelling rather than shared geography. Accounts of persecution, migration, and loss became essential tools for preserving continuity. Through narrative, past experience was translated into guidance for present decision making.

The cumulative effect of war and displacement was not uniform erosion of identity. Rather, these experiences intensified reflection on what it meant to choose the church. Faith could no longer be sustained solely through inherited practice. Individuals were compelled to articulate belief in contexts where communal reinforcement was fragile or absent.

In the broader formation of Mennonite identity, war and migration functioned as catalysts for reinterpretation. They exposed the limits of separation while reinforcing the importance of conscience and commitment. Mennonite history thus reflects not withdrawal from the world but repeated negotiation with it, shaped by conflict and adaptation.

Through displacement, Mennonites carried their tradition across borders and generations. Identity became portable, sustained through memory, narrative, and deliberate choice. War tested the resilience of voluntary faith, while migration demonstrated its capacity to endure beyond place.

Endnotes for Chapter 16

[1] Dyck, Cornelius J. *An Introduction to Mennonite History.* Scottdale, PA: Herald Press, 1993.
[2] Smith, C. Henry. *The Story of the Mennonites.* Revised by Cornelius Krahn. Newton, KS: Mennonite Publishing Office, 1950.
[3] Klassen, Pamela E. *Going by the Moon and the Stars: Stories of Two Russian Mennonite Women.* Waterloo, ON: Wilfrid Laurier University Press, 1994.
[4] Peters, Gerald, ed. *Diary of Anna Baerg, 1916-1924.* Winnipeg: CMBC Publications, 1988.

Chapter 17: Inheriting a Religious Past

Mennonite identity is shaped not only by belief and practice but by inheritance. From childhood, individuals are introduced to a collective past marked by persecution, migration, and deliberate faith. This inheritance does not function as a static tradition but as an interpretive framework through which individuals understand their place within the community and the broader world.

Children raised in Mennonite communities encounter history as lived memory rather than distant record. Stories of martyrdom, exile, and survival are transmitted through family narratives, worship, and education. These accounts emphasize endurance, faithfulness, and sacrifice, presenting history as morally instructive rather than merely informative. The past becomes a source of identity that precedes personal choice.[1]

This inheritance produces both continuity and tension. Shared memory fosters belonging and coherence while simultaneously complicating the ideal of voluntary faith. Individuals are taught that belief must be chosen even as they are formed within a culture that renders certain choices normative. Navigating this tension becomes a central task of identity formation.

> "Little by little, I was sifting out what was Mennonite, never consciously but sort of like getting a tan. You find yourself turning browner, but are never aware of it when it happens."[2]

> "Becoming a Mennonite means being baptized and joining a Mennonite church… more than eating traditional foods and speaking Low German."[3]

Historical consciousness is reinforced through naming practices, language retention, and genealogical awareness. Mennonite families often preserve surnames across generations, creating tangible links between contemporary individuals and historical narratives. Awareness of ancestry strengthens identification with communal experience, making abstract history personal and immediate.

Education plays a significant role in shaping inherited identity. Mennonite schools and religious instruction emphasize historical narrative alongside theological teaching. Accounts of persecution and migration are presented as foundational moments that explain present practices and values. These narratives legitimize separation from broader society and reinforce commitment to voluntary faith.

Memoirs and diaries serve as bridges between generations. Through personal writing, individuals document experiences that might otherwise be lost. These texts allow descendants to engage directly with the voices of predecessors, encountering faith as lived rather than prescribed. In doing so, they humanize history and complicate idealized representations of the past.[2]

Inherited identity does not guarantee acceptance. Many Mennonite narratives describe periods of resistance or ambivalence toward communal expectations. Individuals struggle with the weight of tradition, questioning whether adherence reflects genuine belief or social conformity. These struggles underscore the ongoing relevance of choice within a culture shaped by inheritance.

The process of inheriting a religious past is influenced by migration and assimilation. In pluralistic societies, Mennonite identity competes with alternative affiliations. Exposure to diverse beliefs and lifestyles intensifies reflection on tradition and commitment. For some, this exposure leads to renewed engagement. For others, it prompts departure from the community.

Departure does not necessarily sever connection to the past. Former members often retain a sense of cultural affiliation, shaped by early experiences and shared memory. This persistence suggests that Mennonite identity encompasses both belief and cultural formation, complicating distinctions between religious and social belonging.

Gender influences how inheritance is experienced and transmitted. Women, often responsible for domestic education and caregiving, play a central role in preserving narrative continuity. Through storytelling, ritual, and daily practice, they embed historical consciousness within family life. Men, frequently positioned as public representatives of faith, transmit identity through leadership and instruction. These complementary roles reflect broader patterns within Mennonite society.

The act of inheritance also involves reinterpretation. Each generation encounters new circumstances that challenge established understandings. Economic change, political shifts, and cultural integration require reassessment of how historical principles apply to contemporary life. This process ensures that identity remains dynamic rather than fossilized.

In this context, choosing the church becomes an act informed by memory rather than detached from it. Individuals draw upon inherited narratives as resources for decision making, even as they assert personal agency. The past does not dictate belief but frames the terms through which belief is understood.

Mennonite identity thus emerges as a dialogue between inheritance and choice. History provides continuity, while conversion affirms agency. Together, they sustain a tradition defined not by coercion but by repeated acts of commitment across generations.

Endnotes for Chapter 17

[1] Dyck, Cornelius J. *An Introduction to Mennonite History.* Scottdale, PA: Herald Press, 1993.
[2] Wiebe, Katie Funk. *The Storekeeper's Daughter: A Memoir.* Scottdale, PA: Herald Press, 1997, pg 42.
[3] Klassen, Pamela E. Going by the Moon and the Stars: Stories of Two Russian Mennonite Women. Waterloo, ON: Wilfrid Laurier University Press, 1994, pg. 95.

Conclusion: Continuity Without Coercion

The history traced in this study reveals a religious tradition shaped less by institutional continuity than by repeated acts of decision. From the earliest Anabaptist rejection of infant baptism to later Mennonite practices of discipline, nonresistance, and communal memory, the defining feature of Mennonite identity has been the insistence that faith must be chosen rather than imposed.

This insistence emerged within a historical context that offered little room for voluntary belief. In early modern Europe, church membership was inherited and enforced, binding individuals to civic authority as well as religious practice. Anabaptist refusal to accept this arrangement transformed baptism into an act of defiance and belief into a matter of conscience. The resulting persecution clarified the cost of dissent and reinforced the conviction that coercion undermined faith rather than preserved it.

Mennonite identity developed through adaptation rather than uniformity. The movement survived not by consolidating power or enforcing orthodoxy but by cultivating internal discipline and communal accountability. Separation from the state, nonresistance, and voluntary membership functioned as practical responses to historical constraint. These commitments were refined through crisis, particularly in the aftermath of Münster, when the dangers of enforced belief became unmistakable.

Division within the Mennonite tradition functioned less as a failure of unity than as a structural consequence of commitments that rejected enforced conformity in matters of faith. Without centralized authority, communities responded to disagreement through separation rather than coercion. While such divisions often produced fragmentation, they also preserved the possibility of conscience-driven faith.

Personal narratives illuminate how these historical principles are internalized. Memoirs and diaries demonstrate that choosing the church is rarely a singular event. Conversion unfolds through struggle, doubt, and negotiation between inherited identity and personal conviction. These narratives situate individual decisions within collective memory, reinforcing the link between past experience and present belief.

War, displacement, and migration further complicated this relationship. As Mennonites encountered new political and social environments, inherited practices required reinterpretation. Faith could no longer rely solely on communal reinforcement but demanded renewed articulation. In these contexts, voluntary belief became both more difficult and more deliberate.

The persistence of Mennonite identity across centuries and continents suggests that continuity does not depend on coercive authority. Instead, it emerges from shared memory, disciplined practice, and repeated affirmation of belief. Mennonites have sustained a tradition defined not by uniformity but by commitment, shaped through historical experience rather than institutional dominance.

This study has not sought to evaluate Mennonite belief or to advocate its practices. Rather, it has examined the conditions under which a voluntary religious tradition emerged and endured. In tracing Anabaptist origins, Mennonite adaptation, and narrative self understanding, the book has focused on how faith was constructed in opposition to compulsion.

Choosing the church remains a defining act within Mennonite history, not as an abstract ideal but as a lived response to constraint, loss, and change. Through that choice, Mennonites articulated a vision of religious life grounded in conscience and sustained without force. Their history demonstrates how belief can persist without coercion and how identity endures through memory, discipline, and deliberate commitment.

Note on Sources

This book is a work of historical synthesis and interpretation. It draws primarily on established secondary scholarship in Anabaptist and Mennonite history, as well as on published memoirs, diaries, and autobiographical writings produced within Mennonite communities. It does not present original archival research. Rather, it brings together historical analysis and narrative sources to examine how the idea of voluntary faith emerged, was sustained, and was remembered within the Mennonite tradition.

The historical framework of this study relies on classic works of Mennonite historiography, including texts by Cornelius Dyck, C. Henry Smith, Harold S. Bender, James M. Stayer, John C. Wenger, and William R. Estep. These authors shaped much of the foundational scholarly conversation about Anabaptist origins, persecution, nonresistance, and church discipline. While more recent scholarship has expanded and revised aspects of this field, the sources used here reflect the interpretive traditions that have most strongly influenced Mennonite historical self understanding.

Accounts of early Anabaptism, martyrdom, and persecution are drawn from scholarly syntheses rather than from trial records or archival documents. References to figures such as Augustine, Martin Luther, and Menno Simons rely on their writings as they are presented and analyzed in secondary literature. The goal is not to adjudicate theological debates but to situate Mennonite identity within the historical conditions that shaped religious choice and coercion.

Memoirs, diaries, and conversion narratives play a central role in this study. These sources are treated not as comprehensive representations of Mennonite experience but as interpretive texts that reveal how individuals understood faith, discipline, migration, and belonging. Where personal writings are referenced collectively, they are used illustratively rather than exhaustively, reflecting common themes rather than uniform conclusions.

This book does not seek to offer a definitive account of Mennonite history or belief. Mennonite communities have varied widely across time, geography, and culture, and no single narrative can encompass that diversity. Instead, this study examines recurring patterns of thought and practice related to voluntary faith, community boundaries, and historical memory. It approaches Mennonite identity as dynamic, contested, and continually shaped by the tension between inheritance and choice.

Readers seeking detailed historiographical debate, archival documentation, or comprehensive surveys of all Mennonite groups are encouraged to consult the works cited in the endnotes. The purpose of this book is narrower. It is to explore how a religious tradition formed around the insistence that faith must be chosen, and how that insistence has been remembered, narrated, and reinterpreted across generations.

Works Referenced

Bender, Harold S. Essays on Anabaptist theology and history. Various publications in *Mennonite Quarterly Review,* 1927-1962.

Bekker, Jacob P. *Origin of the Mennonite Brethren Church.* Hillsboro, KS: Mennonite Brethren Publishing House, 1973.

Dyck, Cornelius J. *An Introduction to Mennonite History.* Scottdale, PA: Herald Press, 1993.

Estep, William R. *The Anabaptist Story: An Introduction to Sixteenth-Century Anabaptism.* 3rd ed. Grand Rapids, MI: Eerdmans, 1996.

Hostetler, John A. *Amish Society.* 4th ed. Baltimore: Johns Hopkins University Press, 1993.

Klassen, Pamela E. *Going by the Moon and the Stars: Stories of Two Russian Mennonite Women.* Waterloo, ON: Wilfrid Laurier University Press, 1994.

Lehmann-Haupt, Hellmut. *Gutenberg and the Master of the Playing Cards.* New Haven, CT: Yale University Press, 1966.

Peters, Gerald, ed. *Diary of Anna Baerg, 1916-1924.* Winnipeg: CMBC Publications, 1988.

Ruth, Merle. *The Significance of the Christian Woman's Veiling.* Scottdale, PA: Herald Press, 1973.

Simons, Menno. *The Complete Writings of Menno Simons.* English translations of sixteenth-century works. Accessed January 2000.

Smith, C. Henry. *The Story of the Mennonites.* Revised by Cornelius Krahn. Newton, KS: Mennonite Publishing Office, 1950.

Stayer, James M. *Anabaptists and the Sword*. Rev. ed. Lawrence, KS: Coronado Press, 1976. Reprint, Eugene, OR: Wipf & Stock, 2002.

Wenger, John C. *Glimpses of Mennonite History and Doctrine*. 2nd ed. Scottdale, PA: Herald Press, 1947.

Wiebe, Katie Funk. *The Storekeeper's Daughter: A Memoir*. Scottdale, PA: Herald Press, 1997.

About The Author

Angela Cleveland is a writer with a background in education, organizational leadership, and institutional systems. She spent fifteen years in K-12 education as a school counselor before moving into senior roles in government contracting and operations, where her work has focused on governance, accountability, and how organizations define authority and belonging.

Choosing the Church grew out of her interest in how communities sustain identity through structure, memory, and discipline. Drawing on historical scholarship and Mennonite narrative traditions, the book reflects Cleveland's ongoing engagement with questions of belief, responsibility, and voluntary commitment within enduring institutions.

www.ingramcontent.com/pod-product-compliance
Lightning Source LLC
Chambersburg PA
CBHW071232090426
42736CB00014B/3057